Over-the-Top Animals

Biggest Bear

By Suzane Nguyen

BLASTOFF! BEGINNERS,
AN IMPRINT OF
BELLWETHER MEDIA
BY FLUTTERBEE

Blastoff! Beginners are developed by literacy experts and educators to meet the needs of early readers. These engaging informational texts support young children as they begin reading about their world. Through simple language and high frequency words paired with crisp, colorful photos, Blastoff! Beginners launch young readers into the universe of independent reading.

Sight Words in This Book

a	have	more	the	they
are	help	see	their	to
big	in	some	them	
get	it	than	these	

This edition first published in 2027 by Bellwether Media, Inc.

Text copyright © 2027 by Bellwether Media, Inc. All rights reserved. No part of this publication may be reproduced, stored in any retrieval system, or transmitted in any form or by any means, electronic, mechanical, photocopying, recording, or otherwise, without written permission of the publisher.

BLASTOFF! BEGINNERS and associated logos are trademarks and/or registered trademarks of Bellwether Media, Inc. Bellwether Media is a division of FlutterBee Education Group.

For information regarding permission, write to Bellwether Media, Inc., Attention: Permissions Department, 3500 American Blvd W, Suite 150, Bloomington, MN 55431.

Library of Congress Cataloging-in-Publication Data is available at www.loc.gov or upon request from the publisher.

ISBN: 9798898800079 (hardcover)
ISBN: 9798898801434 (ebook)

Editor: Betsy Rathburn Designer: Laura Sowers

Printed in the United States of America, North Mankato, MN.

Table of Contents

Strong Bites	4
Hungry Eaters	6
Snowy Bears	14
The Biggest Bear	22
Glossary	23
To Learn More	24
Index	24

A polar bear
sees a seal.
It bites!

Hungry Eaters

These **mammals** live in cold places. They are the biggest bears!

They are heavy. Some weigh more than a cow!

They have strong **jaws**. They have big teeth.

jaw

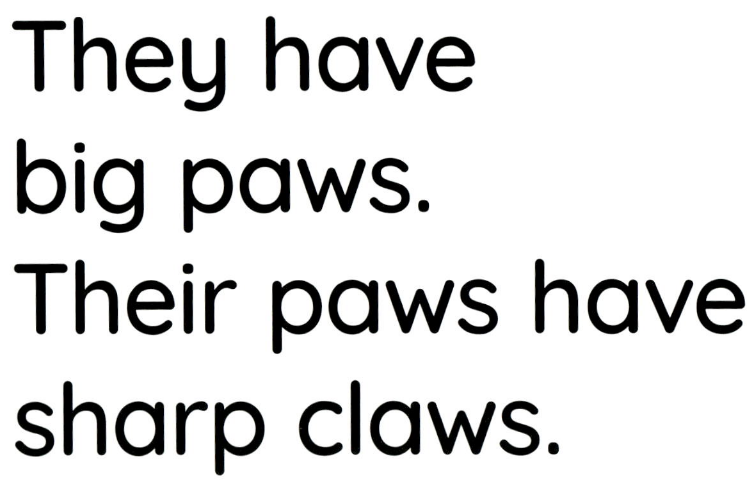

They have
big paws.
Their paws have
sharp claws.

paws

Snowy Bears

Blubber keeps them warm. Their big bodies have a lot!

They swim fast
to get food.
Big paws help.

They hunt
big animals.
Their big teeth
bite hard!

These bears
rule the ice!

The Biggest Bear

Body Parts

Using Their Size

keep warm

swim fast

bite big animals

Glossary

body fat that keeps polar bears warm

strong bones that let animals bite

warm-blooded animals that have hair and feed their young milk

To Learn More

ON THE WEB

FACTSURFER

Factsurfer.com gives you a safe, fun way to find more information.

1. Go to www.factsurfer.com.
2. Enter "biggest bear" into the search box and click 🔍.
3. Select your book cover to see a list of related content.

Index

bites, 4, 18
blubber, 14
claws, 12
jaws, 10, 11
mammals, 6
paws, 12, 13, 16
teeth, 10, 18
weight, 8

The images in this book are reproduced through the courtesy of: Alexey Seafarer, front cover, pp. 22, 23 (mammals); JackF, p. 3; ondrejprosicky, pp. 4, 6-7, 14-15, 23 (blubber); Gabrielle, pp. 4-5, 22 (bite big animals); ManoStudioArt, p. 6; Rixie, pp. 8-9, 12-13; elizalebedewa, pp. 10-11; Nagel Photography, p. 12; Alexey_Seafarer, pp. 16-17; Ellen Goff/ Ellen B Goff/ SuperStock, pp. 18-19; Vaclav, pp. 20-21, 22 (keep warm); Steven Kazlowski/ Left Eye Productions, Inc./ SuperStock, p. 22 (swim fast); Paul Souders/ Danita Delimont, p. 23 (jaws).